Preface

The **Fundamentals of Computer Networks** course (BCS-041) in the IGNOU BCA program plays a pivotal role in laying the groundwork for students to understand the essential concepts of modern communication systems. In today's digital era, where data transmission and networking are integral to nearly every technological operation, a solid grasp of networking principles is crucial for aspiring IT professionals.

"IGNOU BCA Fundamentals of Computer Networks Previous Year Unsolved Papers BCS 041" has been carefully compiled to serve as an effective academic resource for students preparing for this core course. This book offers a rich collection of unsolved question papers from previous examinations, providing learners with an opportunity to engage with actual exam content and enhance their comprehension of key topics such as network architectures, the OSI and TCP/IP models, IP addressing, routing techniques, transmission media, and network protocols.

The unsolved nature of these papers is intended to promote active learning and independent problem-solving. By attempting these questions, students can evaluate their understanding, identify areas of improvement, and build the confidence needed to excel in examinations. Additionally, this resource helps students simulate the exam environment, improving their time management and analytical thinking skills.

Beyond exam preparation, this book is also valuable for educators and trainers who wish to design mock tests, assignments, or classroom discussions based on real exam questions.

We extend our sincere appreciation to the students, faculty members, and reviewers whose contributions and feedback have played a significant role in shaping this compilation. We hope that this book becomes a reliable study companion and a stepping stone toward academic and professional success in the ever-evolving field of computer networks.

Table of Contents

BCS-041

BCA (REVISED)

Chapter 1: Term-End Examination, June- 2013

BCS-041 : FUNDAMENTAL OF COMPUTER NETWORKS

Time: 3 hours

Maximum Marks: 100

Note : Question number **1** is **compulsory.** Answer **any** three question from the rest.

1. (a) Write any four differences between analog and digital systems. 4

(b) Justify the statement "Slotted ALOHA achieves double efficiency thsan pure ALOHA".6

(c) How is CRC code used for error detection in digital networks? Give an example to illustrate your answer. 5

(d) Compare and contrast between "Peer to Peer" and "Client Server" Networking. 5

(e) Explain the count to infinity problem with help of an example. 5

(f) Define silly window syndrome at transport layer? Explain. 5

(g) Write any five advantages of frame relay over X.25 architecture. 5

(h) Differentiate between public-key and private-key cryptography. 5

2. (a) What is MD5? Write the steps for MD5 algorithm. 10

(b) Compare 1G, 2G and 3G wireless generations based on following criteria: 10

(i) Communication method

(ii) Modulation Technique

(iii) Services

(iv) Channel Assignment

3. (a) Discuss distance vector routing with help of a subnet topology. Discuss what are different matrices used in the distance vector routing algorithm. 10

(b) What are the various methods in HTTP? Explain the use of any four methods. 10

4. (a) Write the role of Data link layer in OSI model. Explain the services and functions provided by Data link layer. Also, explain the importance of its sublayers. 10

(b) Explain the importance and functions of layer 2 and layer 3 switches. Also, write advantages and disadvantage of each. 10

5. Write a short notes on the following: 20

(a) RSA algorithm

(b) IP address classes

(c) Fiber optic cables

(d) Time Division Multiplexing

BCS-041

BCA (REVISED)

Chapter 2: Term-End Examination, December 2013

BCS-041 : FUNDAMENTAL OF COMPUTER NETWORKS

Time : 3 hours

Maximum Marks : 100

Note : Question number **1** is **compulsory.** Answer **any three** questions from the rest.

1. (a) What is the need of modulation? Differentiate between analog and frequency modulation. 5

(b) Compare and contrast between Synchronous and Asynchronous transmission using an example for each. 5

(c) What is frequency division multiplexing? Write its advantages and disadvantages. 5

(d) What are the different considerations while choosing a topology for a network ? 4

(e) Why network models are divided into layers? Write the similarities between TCP/IP and OSI model. 5

(f) Explain the working of ARP and RARP. 6

(g) What are gateways? Explain the importance of gateways in networking. 5

(h) What is cell sectoring in wireless networking? State its type. 5

2. (a) Assume message M= 1010101010 bits and generator G =10001 bits. Explain, how CRC is used for error detection using above message bits and generator bits. 10

(b) Explain the working of link state routing algorithm using an example. 10

3. (a) Discuss the functions performed by SNMP for network management. 10

(b) Write the working of Selective Repeat method. Also, compare it with GO-Back –N using example. 10

4. (a) Write an advantages and one disadvantages of the following : 10

(i) Hub

(ii) Bridge

(iii) Repeater

(iv) Modem

(v) Switch

(b) Write the steps of RSA algorithm. Assume two primary numbers p = 3 and q =11, use RSA algorithm to calculate encryption and decryption keys. 10

5. Write a short notes on the following: 20

(a) Code Division Multiplexing

(b) Frame Relay

(c) Slotted ALOHA

(d) Multi - mode fiber optics

BCS-041

BCA (REVISED)

Chapter 3: Term-End Examination, June- 2014

BCS-041 : FUNDAMENTAL OF COMPUTER NETWORKS

Time : 3 hours

Maximum Marks : 100

Note : Question no. **1** is **compulsory.** Attempt **any three** questions from the rest.

1. (a) What are the two sublayers of data link layer? Explain the characteristics of these layers.7

(b) Differentiate between parallel and serial communication using an example for each. 6

(c) Discuss the importance of DHCP, BOOTP and SNMP at Application layer of TCP/IP model. 6

(d) How transport layer of OSI model provide flow control to improve the issue of congestion in the data transfer? 8

(e) Explain the parity bit method used for error detection. Suppose a bit sequence 100110011 is received. Assume odd parity bit method is used, find whether it has been received correctly or not. 8

(f) How are the number of twists in the UTP cable related to its performance? 5

2. (a) Compare and contrast between Amplitude and phase modulation techniques. Discuss the limitations of each. 10

(b) Assume a 10 bit sequence is 101110110 and a divisor (polynomial) is 1101. Calculate the CRC. 10

Note :- show all steps and calculation.

3. (a) Explain the importance of Time Division Multiplexing (TDM). What are the application of TDM? Also, write its disadvantages (if any). 10

(b) Discuss the ATM service classes and QoS (Quality of Service) parameters of each class. 10

4. (a) Differentiate between IPv4 and IPv6. Also, discuss the need of IP v6. 10

(b) Write the drawbacks of transparent fragmentation. Also, discuss Non-transparent fragmentation method. 10

5. Write short notes on the following : 20

(a) IEEE 802.3

(b) RSA

(c) 3G

(d) CDMA

BCS-041
BACHELOR OF COMPUTER APPLICATIONS
(Revised)

Chapter 3: Term-End Examination, December- 2014

BCS-041 : FUNDAMENTALS OF COMPUTER NETWORKS

Time : 3 hours
Maximum Marks : 100
Note : Question no. **1** is **compulsory.** Attempt any **three questions** from the rest.

1. (a) Differentiate between single mode and multi mode optical Fiber. 8
(b) What is count-to-infinity problem in distance vector routing protocol? How does it happen? Explain with an example. 10
(c) Define angle modulation. What are its types? Discuss the limitations of angle modulation.7
(d) Calculate the CRC for bit sequence 1101011011 and generator polynomial is 10011. 10
Note : Show all steps and calculation.
(e) What is Ad hoc Wireless Communication System? Explain. 5
2. (a) Write the steps for Message Digest 5 (MD5) algorithm. 10
(b) Explain the importance of Sliding Window Protocol. Also, list the types of sliding window techniques. 10
3. (a) What is NIC? Write the techniques used by NIC for data transfer. 8
(b) What are the advantages and disadvantages of bridges? 8
(c) Find the class of following IPv4 addresses : 4
(i) 193.14.56.22
(ii) 226.11.14.27
(iii) 134.11.27.13
(iv) 252.5.15.111
4. (a) What is ICMP? Discuss the ICMP message categories. Also, give at least two examples of each ICMP message category. 10
(b) Differentiate between pure ALOHA and slotted ALOHA. Give formulas for their throughput. 10

5. Write short notes on the following : 20
(a) CSMA/CD
(b) Layer 2 Switch
(c) Frame Relay
(d) OSI Model

BCS-041

BACHELOR OF COMPUTER APPLICATIONS

(BCA) (Revised)

Chapter 4: Term-End Examination, June- 2015

BCS-041 : FUNDAMENTALS OF COMPUTER NETWORKS

Time : 3 hours

Maximum Marks : 100

Note : Question no. **1** is **compulsory.** Attempt **any three** questions from the rest. Use of calculators is allowed.

1. (a) Why is serial data transmission faster than parallel data transmission? Explain. 5

(b) What is better for computer communication — analog or digital? Justify your answer. 5

(c) Why are 'Hash functions' called 'one-way functions'? Explain. 5

(d) Differentiate between SVC and PVC of X.25. 5

(e) Write the steps of Distance Vector Routing Algorithm. Give an example to show its working. 10

(f) What is Windowing? How is flow control and reliability achieved through windowing at transport layer ? 10

2. (a) Write a difference between pure ALOHA and slotted ALOHA. If the throughput of pure ALOHA is $S = Ge^{-2G}$, show that the maximum throughput (S_{max}) is 0-184. 10

(b) Explain the working of 3-way handshake used in TCP, using a suitable diagram. 10

3. (a) Calculate CRC, if the message is $x^7 + x^5 +$ and the generator polynomial is $x^3 + 1$. 10

(b) Explain the working of ARP using a diagram. How is it different from RARP? Explain. 10

4. (a) Explain RSA algorithm with example. 10

(b) What is the difference between classful addressing and classless addressing? How does classless addressing result in decrease in the table size ? 10

5. Write short notes on the following : 20

(a) Frame Relay

(b) Fiber Optics Cables

(c) IMAP and POP

(d) OSI Mode

BCS-041

BACHELOR OF COMPUTER APPLICATIONS

(BCA) (Revised)

Chapter 5: Term-End Examination, December- 2015

BCS-041 : FUNDAMENTALS OF COMPUTER NETWORKS

Time : 3 hours

Maximum Marks : 100

Note : Question no. **1** is **compulsory.** Attempt **any three** questions from the rest. Use of calculator is allowed.

1. (a) What is count to infinity problem in distance vector routing protocol? How does it happen? Explain with an example. 10

(b) Explain the advantages of Frame Relay over X•25 network. 5

(c) How are switches and hubs different? List at least four differences. 5

(d) What is the role of parallel and serial transmission devices in computer networking? Explain. 5

(e) Differentiate between frequency shift keying and phase shift keying. 5

(f) What is subnetting? What is the subnetwork address, if the destination address is 200.45.34.56 and the subnet mask is 255.255.240.0 ? 5

(g) Compare and contrast between private key and public key cryptography. 5

2. (a) Explain the concept of Go-Back-N sliding window protocol with a suitable example. 10

(b) Calculate CRC, if the message is 110101001 and the generator is 1011. 10

3. (a) Assume two primary numbers p = 7 and q = 19, use RSA algorithm to show the encryption and decryption with a message "6". 10

(b) Explain the functions of various connecting devices in a LAN. 10

4. (a) What is fragmentation? Explain why IPv4 and IPv6 protocol need to fragment some packets. 10

(b) How is connection established and terminated in TCP using three-way handshaking mechanism? Explain. 10

5. Write short notes on the following : 20

(a) ALOHA Protocols

(b) SNMP

(c) MD5

(d) Wireless Generations (1G, 2G and 3G)

BCS-041

BACHELOR OF COMPUTER APPLICATIONS (BCA)

Chapter 5: Term-End Examination, June- 2016

BCS-041 : FUNDAMENTALS OF COMPUTER NETWORKS

Time : 3 hours

Maximum Marks : 100

Note : Question no. **1** is **compulsory.** Attempt **any three** questions from the rest. Use of calculator is allowed.

1. (a) Compare Hub and Switch. Give the advantages and disadvantages of both Hub and Switch. Briefly discuss the functions of layer-2 switch and layer-3 switch. 10

(b) Write the components of Address field in the Frame Relay Protocol Data Unit (PDU). Also, explain the significance of each component. 10

(c) Write the step-by-step working of Link State Routing. Also, compare it with Distance Vector Routing. 10

(d) Discuss the concept of Sliding Window Protocols with the help of an example. Also, explain how piggybacking technique works. 10

2. (a) Explain POP and IMAP. How does POP work? What are the advantages of IMAP over POP? 10

(b) Assume Data frame is 1101011011 and generator polynomial, G(x) is $x^4 + x + 1$. Calculate the transmitted frame using CRC method. 10

3. (a) Compare between CSMA/CD and Ethernet protocol. How does CSMA/CD resolve the problem of line connection? Explain. 10

(b) Draw the format of IP Header and explain the significance of each field. 10

4. (a) Discuss circuit switching and packet switching methods. Also, discuss their merits and demerits. 10

(b) Assume two prime numbers p and q are 3 and 5 respectively. Calculate private key and public key using RSA algorithm. 10

5. Write short notes on the following : 20

(a) ATM Cell

(b) GSM Architecture

(c) OSI Model

(d) Frequency Modulation

BCS-041

BACHELOR OF COMPUTER APPLICATIONS

(BCA) (Revised)

Chapter 6: Term-End Examination, December- 2016

BCS-041 : FUNDAMENTALS OF COMPUTER NETWORKS

Time : 3 hours

Maximum Marks : 100

Note : Question no. **1** is **compulsory.** Attempt **any three** questions from the rest. Use of calculator is allowed.

1. (a) Differentiate between Pure ALOHA and Slotted ALOHA. If the throughput of Slotted ALOHA is $S = Ge^{-G}$, show that the maximum throughput (S_{max}) is 0-368. 10

(b) Discuss the error control techniques used at the data link layer. Also write the step-by-step procedure of GO-BACK-N ARQ method. 10

(c) Differentiate between adaptive and non-adaptive routing. Explain the working of 'Hierarchical Routing' using suitable topological structure and routing table. 10

(d) What is MD5? Write the step-by-step procedure for generating 128-bit MD5, digest. 10

2. (a) Compare between virtual circuits and circuit switching. Also discuss the effect of router failure in virtual circuits. 10

(b) What is ATM Adaptation Layer (AAL)? Explain how routing and switching is done in ATM Networks. 10

3. (a) Write CRC algorithm. Use it to demonstrate the method of error checking. 10

(b) Differntiate between Analog and Digital Modulation. Compare and contrast between ASK, PSK and FSK (digital modulation techniques). 10

4. (a) Write the significance and usage of the following networking devices : 10

(i) Repeaters

(ii) Bridges

(iii) Switches

(iv) Gateways

(v) Network Interface Card

(b) What is IGMP? Draw the header fields of IGMP. Also explain the significance of each field. 10

5. Differentiate between the following : 20

(a) SMTP and FTP

(b) Guided and Unguided Media

(c) OSI and TCP/IP Models

(d) RSA and DES

BCS-041

BACHELOR OF COMPUTER APPLICATIONS

(BCA) (Revised)

Chapter 6: Term-End Examination, June- 2017

BCS-041 : FUNDAMENTALS OF COMPUTER NETWORKS

Time : 3 hours

Maximum Marks : 100

Note : Question no. **1 is compulsory.** Attempt **any three** questions from the rest. Use of calculator is allowed.

1. (a) Find the CRC for the data polynomial 7

$x^9 + x^7 + x^5 + x^2 + 1$

with the generator polynomial $x^3 + x + 1$.

(b) Match the following to one or more layers of the OSI model (write the name of layer(s)) :4

(i) Error correction and Detection

(ii) Running an e-mail application

(iii) Modulation and Encoding

(iv) Routing of packets

(c) What is a problem with PSK? Explain what are 4-QPSK and 8-QPSK. 5

(d) Suppose a class B network uses 20 bits out of 30 bits to define a network address. How many class B networks are possible in this case? 3

(e) What is the reserved bit pattern of the first byte of a class D address class ? 3

(f) The following Figure 1(a) is a subnet with A, B, C, D and E router nodes : 10

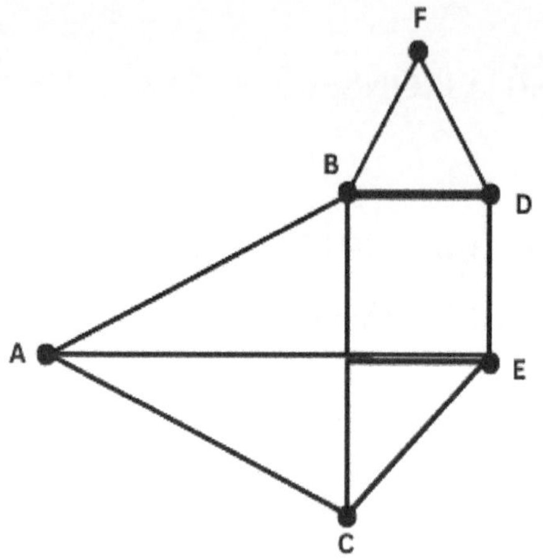

Figure 1(a) : Subnet

In Figure 1(b), the first three columns show the delay vectors received from the neighbours of E(A, C, D).

	A	C	D	E	link
A	0	5	7	10	A
B	10	8	14	-	
C	15	0	21	8	C
D	20	14	0	7	D
E	25	19	28	0	
F	20	25	10	-	

Figure 1(b) : Delay vector

Suppose E has measured its delay to A, C, D as 10, 8, 7 sec respectively. Show how E calculates the delay to B and F routers and through which link.

(g) If p = 7 and q = 11, calculate the encryption key 'e' and the decryption key using RSA algorithm.

8

2. (a) State True/False for the following statements with respect to packet switching : 5

(i) Bandwidth is allocated dynamically.

(ii) Useful for delay sensitive applications.

(iii) Not economical as it needs a dedicated circuit.

(iv) Packet needs to be re-transmitted every time it gets lost.

(v) Overhead is more because every packet is required to carry address.

(b) Compare Bus topology and Star topology with respect to the following parameters : 6

(i) .Central point of failure

(ii) Cable size

(iii) Maintenance and installation cost

(iv) Performance of a system by adding extra cost

(c) Briefly describe the following major access technologies in LAN : 6

(i) CSMA

(ii) Token Passing

(d) Give any two reasons for using a layered protocol. 3

3. (a) How does HTTP protocol work ? 4

(b) Write the throughput expression of Aloha and Slotted Aloha. Also plot load vs throughput graph of the above protocol. 6

(c) Explain hierarchical routing with the help of an example. 6

(d) How does TCP manage loss and duplication of packets?

4

4. (a) Explain the slow start process to manage congestion control at transport layer. 5

(b) What is QoS? Describe any technique to improve QoS. 4

(c) Compare Frame relay and X. 25 with respect to the following parameters : 6

- Data rate
- Flow control and error control mechanisms
- Data link layer feature

(d) State True/False. 5

(i) Bluetooth can support up to 8 devices simultaneously in master/slave mode.

(ii) IEEE 802.3 is a standard of WLAN.

(iii) Every cell in a wireless cellular network has one base station.

(iv) First generation wireless network was intended for voice as well as data.

(v) GSM is used all over the world. .

5 (a) What are the two modes of wireless communication system? Discuss. 6

(b) Draw the GSM architecture and explain the components which manage database. 4

(c) How is block cipher different from stream cipher? Explain with the help of example. 6

(d) Explain the following terms with the help of examples 4

- Non-repudiation
- Encryption

BCS-041

BACHELOR OF COMPUTER APPLICATIONS

(BCA) (Revised)

Chapter 7: Term-End Examination, December- 2017

BCS-041 : FUNDAMENTALS OF COMPUTER NETWORKS

Time : 3 hours

Maximum Marks : 100

Note : Question no. **1** is **compulsory.** Answer **any three** questions from the rest.

1. (a) Find CRC for the data polynomial $x^5+ x^4+ x^2+ 1$ with generator polynomial $x^3+ 1$. 7

(b) Match the following to one or more layers of the OSI model. (Write the name(s) of layer(s))

(i) Running FTP applications 4

(ii) Managing congestion control

(iii) Fragmentation and reassembly of packets

(iv) Encryption/Decryption

(c) How is sampling done from analog signals? Explain through an illustration. 6

(d) How many networks can each IP address class A, B and C have? Also find the number of hosts per network in each given address class. 6

(e) The following Figure 1(a) is a subnet having six routers A, B, C, D, E and F. 10

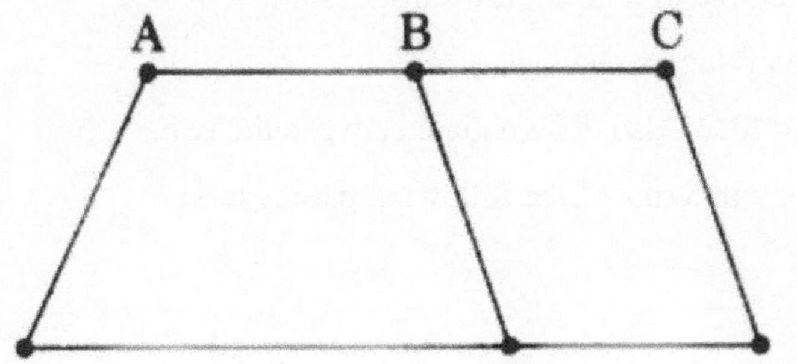

Figure 1(a) : A subnet

The first three columns in Figure 1(b) show the delay vectors received from neighbours of E (i.e., from B, D and F). Suppose that E has also measured its delay to neighbours B, D and F.

To	B	D	F	E: Delay	E: Link
A	4	3	5	-	-
B	0	6	10	6	B
C	8	9	15	-	-
D	12	0	20	8	D
E	16	12	25	0	-
F	20	15	0	7	F

Figure 1(b) : Delay vectors

Show how the router E calculates its delay to A and C.

(f) What is a Congestion Control Mechanism? Discuss slow start phase of TCP's congestion control mechanism through an illustration. 7

2. (a) State True/False. 5

(i) Data transmission has a high signal quality in an analog system compared to a digital system.

(ii) In synchronous transmission, there is no use of start and stop bits.

(iii) In comparison to asynchronous communication, synchronous communication has higher speeds.

(iv) Telephone/mobile conversation is an example of half duplex transmission.

(v) Walkie-talkie device -is an example of half duplex channel.

(b) What do 10 Base T and 100 Base T stand for? Also differentiate between the two. 5

(c) Compare ring topology and mesh topology in terms of the following parameters: 6

(i) Requirement of cable

(ii) Reliability

(iii) Performance of a network by adding extra nodes

(d) How do ARP and RARP work? 4

3. (a) What are the important features of an ATM switch? 4

(b) What is Count-to-Infinity Problem? Explain. 6

(c) Discuss the following in context of network management : 6

(i) Configuration management

(ii) Accounting management

(d) Explain the multiplicative decrease process with respect to congestion control. 4

4. (a) What is Silly Window Syndrome? What are the proposed solutions to this syndrome ? 6

(b) What are the two categories of ICMP messages? Give two examples of each. 6

(c) Differentiate between virtual circuit and datagram. 3

(d) Explain the following features of IPv6 : 5

(i) Tunnelling

(ii) Dual IP stack

5. (a) (i) Given the network address 125.0.0.0., find the class, the block and the range of the address. 3

(ii) How can we prove that we have 2,147,483,648 addresses in Class A? 2

(b) What are the pros and cons of a wireless communication system? 5

(c) How does MD5 message digest algorithm work? Explain. 6

(d) Explain the following terms : 4

- Decryption
- Cryptography

BCS-041

BACHELOR OF COMPUTER APPLICATIONS

(BCA) (Revised)

Chapter 8: Term-End Examination, June- 2018

BCS-041 : FUNDAMENTALS OF COMPUTER NETWORKS

Time : 3 hours

Maximum Marks . 100

Note : Question no. **1** is **compulsory.** Answer **any three** questions from the rest. Use of calculator is allowed.

1. (a) Given data frame is 1101011011 and generator polynomial $G(x) = x^4 + x + 1$. Derive the transmitted frame using CRC method. Write all the steps involved in the process. 10

(b) Explain each step of the process for generating 128 bit MD5 digest from any given number and key. 10

(c) Differentiate between Glassful addressing and classless addressing. Explain how classless addressing results in decrease in the table size. 10

(d) Explain how routing and switching is done in ATM Networks. 10

2. (a) Write the importance of Time Division Multiplexing (TDM). What are the applications of TDM? Also write its disadvantages (if any). 10

(b) Discuss the differences between IPv4 and IPv6. Also highlight the need of IPv6. 10

3. (a) Draw and explain connection establishment and termination in TCP using the three-way handshaking method. 10

(b) With the help of an example, explain Go-back-N sliding window protocol. 10

4. (a) Discuss the functions of DHCP and SNMP. 10

(b) Differentiate between circuit switching and virtual circuit. Also explain the effect of router failure in virtual circuits. 10

5. Write short notes on the following : 20

(a) RSA

(b) Fiber Optic Cables

(c) OSI Model

(d) CSMA/CD

BCS-041

BACHELOR OF COMPUTER APPLICATIONS

(BCA) (Revised)

Chapter 8: Term-End Examination, December- 2018

BCS-041 : FUNDAMENTALS OF COMPUTER NETWORKS

Time : 3 hours

Maximum Marks : 100

Note : Question no. **1** is **compulsory.** Attempt **any three** questions from the rest. Use of calculator is allowed.

1. (a) Assume two prime numbers p and q are 17 and 11 respectively. Calculate private key and public key using RSA algorithm. 10

(b) Draw the format of IP header and explain the significance of each field in this header. 10

(c) Compare between CSMA/CD and token passing methods in Ethernet. Also explain how collisions are handled by CSMA/CD. 10

(d) Explain the working of link state routing. Also compare it with distance vector routing. 10

2. (a) Compare Pure ALOHA with Slotted ALOHA. If throughput of Slotted ALOHA is S = Ge-G, show that the maximum throughput (Smax) is 0.368. 10

(b) What is Digital Modulation? Compare and contrast between ASK, PSK and FSK. 10

3. (a) Explain any five network topologies. Give one advantage and one disadvantage of each topology. 10

(b) What is windowing? How are flow control and reliability achieved through windowing at transport layer ? 10

4. (a) What is IGMP? Draw the header fields of IGMP and explain the significance of each field. 10

(b) Compare OSI-reference model with TCP/IP model. 10

5. Write short notes on the following : 20

(a) IP Address Classes

(b) ATM Cell

(c) MD5 Algorithm

(d) POP

(e) IMAP

BCS-041

BACHELOR OF COMPUTER APPLICATIONS

(BCA) (Revised)

Chapter 9: Term-End Examination, June- 2019

BCS-041 : FUNDAMENTALS OF COMPUTER NETWORKS

Time : 3 Hours

Maximum Marks : 100

Note : Question No. **1** is **compulsory.** Attempt **any three** questions from the rest. Use of calculator is allowed.

1. (a) How the number of turns in UTP cable is related to its performance? Why shielding of cable is required? Explain briefly. 7

(b) Explain how a wireless network is configured. 6

(c) Briefly explain X.25 architecture with the help of a diagram. 8

(d) Briefly explain client-server model of network. 5

(e) What is TCP's sliding window? Explain Silly Window Syndrome with the help of a diagram. 7

(f) What is parity bit method for error detection? Suppose a bit sequence 110001010111 is received. Assume odd parity bit method is used. Find whether received bit sequence is correct or not. 7

2. (a) What is IPV 6? Explain its needs. How IPV 6 is better than IPV 4 ? 10

(b) What is count to infinity problem in distance vector routing protocol? How does it happen? Explain briefly. 10

3. (a) What is OSI model? List all the layers of OSI model and also write two functions of each layer. 15

(b) What is problem with PSK? Explain how it may be solved. 5

4. (a) What is Packet Switching? Explain connection less packet switching with the help of a diagrain. 10

(b) What are Quality of Services (QoS) of network? Briefly explain any three parameters of QoS. Also list any two techniques to improve QoS. 10

5. Write short notes on the following: 20

(a) Communication Ports

(b) Multiplexing

(c) Authentication and Privacy

(d) Synchronous and Asynchronous Transmission

BCS-041

BACHELOR OF COMPUTER APPLICATIONS

(BCA) (Revised)

Chapter 9: Term-End Examination, December- 2019

BCS-041 : FUNDAMENTALS OF COMPUTER NETWORKS

Time : 3 Hours

Maximum Marks : 100

Note : Question no. **1** is **compulsory.** Attempt **any three** questions from the rest.

1. (a) Explain two modes of wireless communication. 6

(b) What is Synchronous Communication? Briefly explain its advantages and disadvantages. 6

(c) What is Star Topology? Explain its advantages and disadvantages. Also describe use of switch in star topology. 7

(d) Explain leaky bucket algorithm for congestion control. Also list its advantages and disadvantages. 8

(e) What is Social Networking? Explain its advantages. 6

(f) Explain how Authentication can be proved through, Identification. 7

2. (a) Differentiate between public key cryptography and private-key cryptography. Assume two prime numbers p and q are 13 and 17 respectively. Calculate private key and public key using RSA algorithm. 10

(b) Calculate CRC, if the message is 110101001 and the generator is 1011. 10

3. (a) What is Transparent Fragmentation 2 How it is different from non-transparent fragmentation method? Explain. 8

(b) What is Frame Relay? Explain network architecture of frame relay with the help of a diagram. Also draw format of frame. 12

4. (a) What is DNS 2 Explain its advantages. 5

(b) What is Internet Group Message Protocol (IGMP)? Briefly explain types of query messages in IGMP. 8

(c) What is E-Governance? Explain any three characteristics of E-Governance. 7

5. Write short notes on the following : 20

(a) Applications of Computer Networking

(b) Working of Asynchronous Transfer Mode (ATM)

(c) Electronic Mail

(d) Network Interface Card (NIC)

BCS-041

BACHELOR OF COMPUTER APPLICATION

(BCA) (Revised)

Chapter 9: Term-End Examination, June- 2020

BCS-041 : FUNDAMENTALS OF COMPUTER NETWORKS

Time : 3 Hours

Maximum Marks : 100

Note: Question number **1** is **compulsory.** Answer **any three** questions from the rest. Use of calculator is allowed

1. (a) Compare Analog and Digital communication systems. Give example of each. 5

(b) What is frequency modulation? Give two advantages and two disadvantages of frequency modulation. 5

(c) What is multiplexing? Briefly discuss the importance of multiplexing. List the basic multiplexing techniques. 5

(d) Differentiate between OSI and TCP/IP model. 5

(e) Discuss the role of switch as a inter networking king device. Compare layer 2 switch with layer 3 switch. 5

(f) Compare circuit switching with virtual circuit and Datagram. 5

(g) What is Block Cipher? Give two advantages and two disadvantages of Block Cipher. 5

(h) Explain Data Encryption Standard (DBS) with suitable example. 5

2. (a) Discuss OSI reference model with suitable block diagram. Briefly discuss the function of each layer in OSI reference model. 10

(b) Explain the following Digital modulation techniques: 6

(i) Amplitude Shift Keying

(ii) Frequency Shift Keying

(iii) Phase Shift keying

(c) Compare synchronous and Asynchronous transmission. Give advantage and disadvantage of both. 4

3 . (a) Draw block diagram to show the classification of Medium access control techniques. 5

(b) What is Address Resolution Protocol (ARP)? Discuss the working of ARP with a suitable block diagram. 5

(c) What is the function of Datalinf Layer? Briefly discuss the role of two sublayers of Datalink layer. 5

(d) What do 10 base T and 100 Base T stand for? Also differentiate between the two. 5

4. (a) Compare Adaptive Routing algorithms with Non-Adaptive Routing algorithms. 5

(b) Discuss the leaky bucket algorithm. Give its advantages and disadvantages. 5

(c) What is the need of data fragmentation? Compare Transparent fragmentation with Non-transparent fragmentation. 5

(d) Explain silly window syndrome. Briefly discuss the solution to silly window syndrome. 5

5. Write short notes on following: 20

(i) Frame Relay

(ii) GSM architecture

(iii) MD 5

(iv) Cryptanalysis

BCS-041

BACHELOR OF COMPUTER APPLICATIONS

(B.C.A.) (REVISED)

Chapter 9: Term-End Examination, December- 2020

BCS-041 : FUNDAMENTALS OF COMPUTER NETWORKS

Time : 3 Hours

Maximum Marks : 100

Note : (i) Question number **1** is **compulsory.** Attempt **any three** questions from the rest. (ii) Use of calculator is allowed.

1. (a) Compare serial and parallel transmission. Give advantages and disadvantages of both. 5

(b) What is Amplitude Modulation? Give two advantages and two disadvantages of amplitude modulation. 5

(c) What do you understand by the term sampling in digital communication? Compare analog to digital conversion with digital to analog conversion. 5

(d) Give at least two similarities between OSI and TCP/IP models. 5

(e) What is Random access protocol? Compare throughout of pure and slotted ALOHA. 5

(f) Briefly discuss the term "classful addressing". Give disadvantage of classful addressing. Given the network address 17.0.0.0, find the class, the block and the range of address. 5

(g) What is stream cipher? Give two advantages and two disadvantages of stream cipher. 5

(h) Compare symmetric and asymmetric cryptography. 5

2. (a) Briefly discuss the functions of various layers involved in TCP/IP model, also mention the protocols defined under each layer. 10

(b) Briefly discuss the following types of multiplexing : 10

(i) Frequency division multiplexing

(ii) Time division multiplexing

(iii) Code division multiplexing

(iv) Space division multiplexing

3. (a) What is round robin technique for transmission? How does polling differ from token passing ? 5

(b) What are the major functions of transport layer? How transmission control protocol differs from user datagram protocol ? 5

(c) Briefly discuss the term Cyclic Redundancy Check (CRC). Find CRC for the data polynomial $x^5 + x^4 + x^2 + 1$ with generator polynomial $x^3 + 1$. 10

4. (a) What is distance vector routing? Briefly discuss the problem of distance vector routing. 5

(b) Compare token bucket algorithm with leaky bucket algorithm. 5

(c) What do you understand by the term Quality of Services (QoS). Discuss the techniques to improve QoS. 5

(d) Differentiate between ICMP and IGMP. 5

5. Write short notes on the following : 20

(i) X.25 Architecture

(ii) CDMA

(iii) RSA

(iv) Public and private key cryptography

BCS-041

BACHELOR OF COMPUTER APPLICATIONS

(BCA) (Revised)

Chapter 9: Term-End Examination, June- 2021

BCS-041 : FUNDAMENTALS OF COMPUTER NETWORKS

Time : 3 hours

Maximum Marks : 100

Note : Question no. **1** is **compulsory.** Attempt **any three** questions from the rest. Use of calculator is allowed.

1. (a) Which type of communication, digital or analog, is better for computers? Justify your answer. 5

(b) What are 'Hash functions'? Why are they called 'One-way functions'? Explain. 5

(c) Compare SVC and PVC of X·25 architecture. 5

(d) Why is serial data transmission faster than parallel data transmission? Explain. 5

(e) How are the number of twists in the UTP cable related to its performance? 5

(f) Name the two sublayers of Data Link Layer, and explain the characteristics of these layers 5

(g) Explain Silly Window Syndrome, with the help of a diagram. 5

(h) Briefly discuss the problem with PSK and explain its possible solution. 5

2. (a) Compare and contrast the amplitude modulation and phase modulation techniques. Discuss the limitations of each. 10

(b) Explain RSA algorithm with example. 10

3. (a) Explain the working of 3-way handshake used in TCP, using a suitable diagram. 10

(b) Discuss the ATM service classes and QoS (Quality of Services) parameters of each class. 10

4. (a) Calculate the CRC for a 10 bit sequence 1010011110 with a divisor of 1011. Note : Show all steps and calculations 10

(b) Compare Time Division Multiplexing (TDM) and Frequency Division Multiplexing (FDM). Give the advantage and disadvantage (if any) of both TDM and FDM. 10

5. Write short notes on the following : 20

(a) CSMA/CD

(b) IEEE 802.3

(c) Frame Relay

(d) OSI Mode

BCS-041

BACHELOR OF COMPUTER APPLICATIONS

(BCA) (REVISED)

Chapter 9: Term-End Examination, December- 2021

BCS-041 : FUNDAMENTALS OF COMPUTER NETWORKS

Time : 3 Hours

Maximum Marks : 100

Note : Question number **1** is **compulsory.** Attempt **any three** questions from the rest. Use of calculator is allowed.

1. (a) Differentiate between parallel and serial communication. Give an example of each. 5

(b) Discuss the importance of DHCP and SNMP at the application layer of TCP/IP model. 5

(c) Compare POP and IMAP. 5

(d) What are Quality of Services (QoS) of network? List any two techniques to improve QoS. 5

(e) What is CRC? Calculate CRC, if the message is x7 + x^5 + ^{1} and the generator polynomial is x^3+ 1. 10

(f) What is classful addressing? How is it different from classless addressing? How does classless addressing result in the decrease of the table size? 10

2. (a) Differentiate between pure ALOHA and slotted ALOHA. If the throughput of pure ALOHA is $S = Ge^{-2G}$, show that the maximum throughput max (S_{max}) is 0.184. 10

(b) What is Windowing? How are flow control and reliability achieved through windowing at transport layer? 10

3. (a) Explain the working of ARP, using a diagram. How does ARP differ from RARP? Explain. 10

(b) Discuss the advantages of IPv6 over IPv4. 5

(c) Discuss the importance of DHCP and BOOTP at the application layer of TCP/IP model. 5

4. (a) Write the step by step working of lmk state routing. Also, compare it with distance vector routing. 10

(b) Write the components of address field in the Frame Relay Protocol Data Unit (PDU). Also, explain the significance of each component. 10

5. Write short notes on the following : 20

(a) Circuit Switching

(b) GSM Architecture

(c) 3G Network(d) Fibre Optic Cables

BCS-041

BACHELOR OF COMPUTER APPLICATIONS

(BCA) (Revised)

Chapter 10: Term-End Examination, June- 2022

BCS-041 : FUNDAMENTALS OF COMPUTER NETWORKS

Time : 3 hours

Maximum Marks : 100

Note : Question no. **1** is **compulsory.** Attempt **any three** questions from the rest. Use of calculator is allowed.

1. (a) Briefly discuss the term CRC. Determine the CRC for the data polynomial $X^5 + X^4 + X^2 + 1$ with generator polynomial $X^3 + 1$. 7

(b) Explain how routing and switching is done in ATM network. 10

(c) Differentiate between Classful addressing and Classless addressing. Explain how classless addressing results in decrease in table size. 10

(d) What is a Congestion Control Mechanism? Discuss slow start phase of TCP congestion control mechanism through an illustration. 7

(e) What do 10Base-T and 100Base-T stand for? Also, differentiate between the two. 6

2. (a) Compare Ring topology and Mesh topology, in terms of the following parameters : 6

(i) Requirement of cable

(ii) Reliability

(iii) Performance of network by adding extra nodes

(b) What is Count-to-Infinity problem? Explain. 4

(c) Explain the multiplicative decrease process, with respect to congestion control. 4

(d) What is Silly Window Syndrome? What are the proposed solutions to this syndrome ? 6

3. (a) Answer the following :

(i) Given the network address 125.0.0.0, find the class, the block and the range of the address. 3

(ii) How can we prove that we have 2, 147, 483, 648 addresses in class A ? 2

(b) Discuss the pros and cons of a wireless communication system. 5

(c) How does MD5 message digest algorithm work? Explain. 5

(d) Explain Client-Server model of network, with the help of a diagram. 5

4. (a) Discuss the parity bit method for error detection? Suppose a bit sequence 110001010111 is received. Assume odd parity bit method is used. Find whether received bit sequence is correct or not. 10

(b) Explain X.25 architecture, with the help of a diagram. 10

5. Write short notes on the following : 20

(a) Count-to-Infinity Problem in Distance Vector Routing Protocol

(b) Quality of Service (QoS) of Network

(c) Functions of DHCP

(d) Functions of SNMP

(e) CSMA/CD

BCS-041

BACHELOR OF COMPUTER APPLICATIONS

(BCA) (Revised)

Chapter 10: Term-End Examination, December- 2022

BCS-041 : FUNDAMENTALS OF COMPUTER NETWORKS

Time : 3 hours

Maximum Marks : 100

Note : Question no. **1** is **compulsory.** Attempt **any three** questions from the rest. Use of calculator is allowed.

1. (a) What is MD5 Digest? Explain the steps for the process of generating 128 bit MD5 digest from any given number and key. 10

(b) How is sampling done from analog signals? Explain through an illustration. 7

(c) Given data frame as 1101011011 and generator polynomial $G(x) = x^4 + x + 1$, derive the transmitted frame using CRC method. Write all the steps involved in the process. 10

(d) How many networks can each IP address class A, B and C have? Also find the number of hosts per network in each of the given address class. 6

(e) Discuss the working of ARP and RARP. Also, differentiate between the two. 7

2. (a) Discuss the following in context of network management : 6

(i) Configuration management

(ii) Accounting management

(b) What are the important features of an ATM switch ? 4

(c) What are the two categories of ICMP messages? Give two examples of each. 6

(d) Differentiate between Virtual circuit and Datagram. 4

3. (a) Explain the following features of IPv6 : 5

(i) Tunneling

(ii) Dual IP Stack

(b) What is the problem with PSK? Explain how it may be solved. 5

(c) What is TCP's sliding window? Explain Silly Window Syndrome with the help of a diagram. 10

4. (a) Explain Time Division Multiplexing (TDM). Discuss the advantages and disadvantages of TDM. Also, give applications of TDM. 10

(b) What is Three-way handshaking method? Draw and explain the connection establishment and termination in TCP using Three-way handshaking method. 10

5. (a) Differentiate between the following : 10

(i) Circuit switching and Packet switching

(ii) IPv4 and IPv6

(b) Write short notes on the following : 10

(i) RSA

(ii) OSI Model

BCS-041

BACHELOR OF COMPUTER APPLICATIONS

(BCA) (REVISED)

Chapter 10: Term-End Examination, June- 2023

BCS-041 : FUNDAMENTALS OF COMPUTER NETWORKS

Time : 3 Hours

Maximum Marks : 100

Note : Question number **1** is **compulsory.** Attempt **any three** questions from the rest. Use of calculator is allowed.

1. (a) Differentiate between private key and public key cryptography. Give suitable example of each. 6

(b) Briefly discuss the concept of frequency shift keying and phase shift keying. Give an application of each. 6

(c) What is count to infinity problem in distance vector routing protocol? How does it happen? Explain with an example. 10

(d) Briefly discuss the functions of Layer-2 switch and Layer-3 switch. Compare Switch with Hub. 6

(e) How does pure ALOHA differ from slotted ALOHA? Explain. 6

(f) What are virtual circuits? Discuss the effect of router failure in virtual circuits. 6

2. (a) Differentiate between ARP and RARP. Explain the working of ARP using a diagram. 10

(b) How does classful addressing differ from classless addressing? How does classless addressing result in decrease in the table size? 10

3. (a) Explain the concept Go-Back-N sliding window protocol with a suitable example and diagram. 10

(b) What is Fragmentation? Explain why IPv4 and IPv6 protocols need to fragment some packets. 10

4. (a) Write the step-by-step working of link state routing. Also, compare it with distance vector routing. 10

(b) Discuss the concept of sliding window protocol with the help of an example. Also, explain how piggybacking technique works. 10

5. (a) What is IGMP? Draw the header fields of IGMP. Also, explain the significance of each field. 10

(b) Write the significance and usage of the following networking devices : 10

(i) Repeater

(ii) Bridges

(iii) Switches

(iv) Gateways

(v) Networks interface card

BCS–041

BACHELOR OF COMPUTER APPLICATIONS

(BCA) (REVISED)

Chapter 11: Term-End Examination, December- 2023

BCS-041 : FUNDAMENTALS OF COMPUTER NETWORKS

Time : 3 Hours

Maximum Marks: 100

Note : Question No. **1** is **compulsory.** Answer **any three** questions from the rest. Use of calculator is allowed.

1. (a) What is a Frame Relay? Explain the advantages of Frame Relay over X.25 Network. 6

(b) How are Hubs, Switches and Routers different from each other ? 6

(c) Explain POP and IMAP. What are the advantages of IMAP over POP ? 6

(d) Compare CSMA/CD and Ethernet protocol. 6

(e) How does circuit switching and packet switching differ? Give merits and demerits of both. 6

(f) Write the steps of Distance Vector Routing Algorithm. Show case the working of this algorithm with an example. 10

2. (a) Explain the working of 3-way handshake used in TCP using a suitable diagram. 10

(b) What is Windowing? How are flow control and reliability achieved through windowing at transport layer ? 10

3. (a) List various connecting devices in a LAN. Explain the functioning of each. Also show the interconnectivity between devices with suitable diagram. 10

(b) Briefly discuss the utility of CRC. Calculate CRC if the message is $x^7 + x^5 + 1$ and the generator polynomial is x^3+1. 10

4. (a) Differentiate between Analog and Digital Modulation. Compare and contrast between ASK, PSK and FSK (digital modulation techniques). 10

(b) What is MD5? Write step by step procedure for generating 128 bit MD5 digest. 10

5. (a) Differentiate between adaptive and nonadaptive routing. Explain the working of hierarchical routing using suitable topological structure and routing table. 10

(b) Discuss the error control techniques used at the data link layer. Also write the step-by-step procedure of Go-BACK-N ARQ Method. 10

9 789369 721214

Printed at Repro India Ltd.